A Beginner's Guide to BAG MAKING

20 CLASSIC STYLES EXPLAINED STEP BY STEP

Estelle Zanatta and Marion Grandamme

YOU ARE SO SMART

SEARCH PRESS

Contents

Introduction

We love bags and we love sewing. No fashion collection of ours is complete without the creation of a bag.

Whether clutch or cross-the-shoulder, chic or casual, a bag is a key item in our wardrobe. It accessorizes an outfit and adds another shade of colour to complete a look. We love these daily companions of ours, and so we were delighted to accept the challenge: a book on bags? It's in the bag!

Our main aim has been to explore different kinds of bag and to contribute our small brick to the great wall of creative hobbies, full of ideas and colours. Our book seeks to provide our readers with the skills to make the bags they want. With this book as your guide, you can create your very own signature bag, unique to you: a clutch for evenings out, an everyday bag to take to work, a holdall for shopping trips or a sports bag for when you are off to unwind.

We have drawn on our world and experience, but we have also been inspired by the history of the bag and have sprinkled a few anecdotes throughout the book. We have chosen ten basic shapes that seem most relevant to us. More often than not, these projects have one or two variations that illustrate the diversity of choice when it comes to materials and techniques. Explanations will guide you through the various stages so you do not find yourself with a rubbish bag instead of a handbag! There are plenty of tips to help you along the way. We would recommend starting with the first projects in the book in order to familiarize yourself with the basic techniques. Each project's level of difficulty is given in the header.

We have come up with some simple bags, some practical bags and even some cheeky bags that you can personalize or customize as you like. After a bit of practice you will soon be making the bags of your dreams.

Estelle & Marion

Supplies and materials

- A universal (patchwork) ruler (1)
- Paper scissors and sewing scissors (2): it is always best to keep the two separate so the sewing scissors stay sharp.

- An erasable pen (3): always handy for sewing projects as it disappears under the heat of the iron! You can get refills (4).

- Tailor's chalk (5): an alternative to the erasable pen; better for certain materials or dark coloured fabrics.

- A mechanical pencil (6): go for H leads rather than HB (they are less greasy).

- A thread clipper (7)

- An unpicker (8)

- Pins

- Eyelets (9) and a chain with snap hooks (10): some examples of small hardware items you might need to finish your bags.

- Iron-on interfacing: there are numerous types of thermal interfacing which help bags to stay in shape. We have used thin, medium, thick and semi-rigid (plastified) iron-on interfacing as well as iron-on wadding/batting (11).

- A sewing machine: with a standard presser foot and a zipper foot, needles of different sizes (use 80 for normal fabrics and 90 for heavier ones).

- Thread (12): if you cannot find the exact colour, use a darker one.

- White paper: for copying patterns.

N.B. Zips can differ in type, size, colour, width and tooth colour (plastic, metal, nickel, gold, narrow, wide, etc.).

The list of supplies is given at the start of the instructions for each project.
Feel free to adapt it to match materials you have available.

Glossary and tips

A good sewing lesson is much like a recipe. Before you begin, make sure you have all the ingredients to hand. It is always better to get started when you know you have a few hours ahead of you. Lay out all the ingredients on the table and take an initial look through the instructions.

If you are a novice, you are going to require plenty of patience and concentration, and you will probably need to try it several times to perfect the recipe. You will slowly find the best way of doing things and before you know it you will be a true cordon bleu! If you already know what you are doing, after you have completed some of the projects in the book you might prefer to give free rein to your imagination and sprinkle a few ideas here and there, mixing different projects and peppering the recipes with your own ideas.

THE CUT

The cut is the way a pattern is designed; it defines the shape of the finished bag. It is also the result of cutting the pieces properly: you must cut the fabric in accordance with its grain (the direction of the warp and weft). Cutting advice: stand up, with the point of the scissors downwards, resting on the table. The fabric should barely move when you cut it. Fabric can be pinned to aid cutting.

NOTCHES

Notches are marks on the pattern that need to be transferred to the fabric by cutting nicks with the tips of the scissors. Make sure that all these notches are clearly visible on both fabric and lining. They provide a guide to aligning the different pieces.

MITRING CORNERS

This is bias cutting excess fabric from the seam allowance in order to make corners less bulky. This step means there are fewer layers of fabric.

INTERFACING

This is reinforcement that is ironed on or sewn inside a bag to make it more solid so it holds its shape better. Tips for using iron-on interfacing: use a hot iron, perform a small test sample by pressing the iron down on the interfacing for 30 seconds and if necessary finishing off with a little bit of steam. Iron-on interfacing does sometimes come unstuck. This does not really matter if the edges have been properly secured within the seams.

FACING

The facing is the strip of material that gives the bag an attractive finish round the top inside edge. It can be made by folding over the fabric used for the outside at the top of the bag (extended facing) or cut as a separate pattern piece. Adding a facing allows the lining to be concealed.

TOPSTITCH SEAM

Topstitching helps the material to stay in place. It is often used in hidden areas, particularly for the lining. You press all the seam allowances under the lining and sew 1mm ($^{1}/_{32}$ in) from the edge.

OVERSEWING

When you finish stitching on the machine, sew backwards and forwards for two or three stitches. You can also bring the thread round to the wrong side of the fabric so you don't see the trimmed ends.

SLIPSTITCH

An invisible hand-sewn stitch (aligns the edges of the fabric).

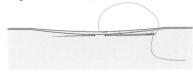

CUSTOMIZING THE PATTERN

The dimensions of the bags can be easily adjusted by making slight changes to the patterns. Tip: trace the pattern onto white paper (always keep the original). Increase or decrease the length, width and/or height. Shift the notches as necessary. As these are geometric shapes you must be able to fit the pieces together (check lengths).

Simple zip – up bag

This two-tone zip-up bag has a removable chain clipped on using snap hooks so that it can be easily slipped inside a bigger bag or carried over the shoulder. You can make other variations; it comes out well in all sorts of fabrics (plain, printed, fine or thick). Note that we have used the same fabric on the outside (right side) and the inside (wrong side) of the bag.

PATTERN PIECES

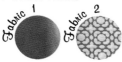

- Front and back panels of the bag (piece No. 1): cut x 2 (*fabric 1*)
- Folded pocket panels front and back (piece No. 2): cut x 2 (*fabric 2 on the fold*)
- Front and back lining panels (piece No. 1): cut x 2 (*fabric 2 wrong side*)
- Loops for the rings (piece No. 3): cut x 2 (*fabric 1*)

SUPPLIES

- 50cm (19¾in) artificial leather, composition 55% polyurethane, 45% viscose (*fabric 1*)
- 50cm (19¾in) pink and white jacquard fabric (*fabric 2*)
- 1 x 25cm (9¾in) nickel (silver) zip, brown or burgundy
- 3 x small 1cm (½in) diameter rings
- 1 nickel and pink tassel
- 1 x 125cm (49¼in) nickel chain
- 2 x nickel snap hooks for the chain
- Burgundy thread, to match the colour of the outside of the bag

A BIT OF HISTORY

The reticule (nineteenth century), or 'small net' is the ancestor of today's handbags. The name refers to the reticulum carried by Roman ladies some 2000 years earlier. This accessory replaced pockets which, with the development of lighter, more tightly fitting clothing, no longer formed a part of ladies' clothing.

The handbag came into its own in the 1920s when women sought a practical solution for the things they had to carry. Sleeves, fitted with internal pockets, had fulfilled this role for some time. But with the invention of the zip fastener by Émile Hermès in 1918, the bag made its definitive entry into the modern era.

METHOD

▸ Cut the pattern pieces from the fabrics and materials.

PUTTING IN A ZIP
step by step

PUTTING IN A ZIP

▸ Place the zip on the front panel (*fabric 1*), right sides together.
▸ Lay the front lining on top, right sides together, sandwiching the zip between the two pieces of fabric, and secure with pins. **(1)**

▸ Stitch using a special zip presser foot. **(2)**

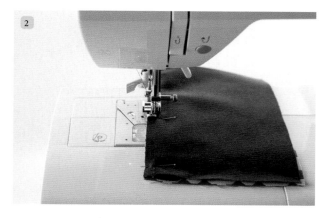

▸ Repeat the two previous steps for the back panels (*fabric 1 and fabric 2*).

▸ Here, seen from above, is what it should look like. **(3)**

▸ Iron on the wrong side without steam.

PREPARING THE RING LOOPS

▸ Turn in 1cm (½in) all along the long edges of the loop pieces.
▸ Fold the pieces lengthways (like bias binding) and iron.
▸ Topstitch along the edges, 1mm ($^1/_{32}$in) from the edge.
▸ Pass each piece through a ring and fold in half to form the loop.

SEWING THE MAIN BODY OF THE BAG

▸ Fold the two pocket panels along the fold lines given on the pattern and place them on the front and back panels respectively. Stitch all round the pieces, 0.5cm (¼in) from the edge, to hold them in place.
▸ Position and sew the two loops, holding the rings on each side (as shown on the pattern).
▸ Sew the front and back together, all round the bag, right sides together.

Take care: do not sew too close to the zip so it is easier to turn the right way out.

SEWING THE LINING

▸ Sew together the front and back of the lining, right sides together, leaving an opening of around 10cm (4in) in the seam at the bottom.
▸ Turn the right way out.
▸ Sew up the bottom of the bag by hand using slipstitch or by topstitching on the machine.

ATTACHING THE CHAIN AND THE TASSEL

▸ Take two pairs of flat-nose pliers; use one to hold the chain in place and the other to pull it open. **(4)**
▸ Insert the snap hook and close again in the same way.
▸ Open the second ring in the same way, pass it through the hole in the zip pull and add the tassel.

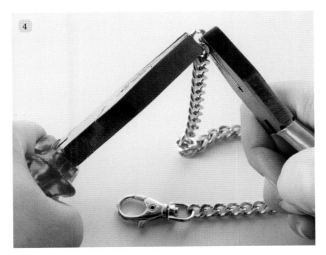

MAKING A
SIMPLE POCKET

step by step

Folded bag

This bag can be carried in your hand or under your arm. The contrast flap highlights the patterned fabric on the front and back of the bag. We have chosen bright, cheerful fabrics to give it some added zing.

PATTERN PIECES

Fabric 1   Fabric 2   Lining

- Front panel of bag (piece No. 1): cut x 1 (*fabric 1*)
- Back panel (piece No. 2): cut x 1 (*fabric 1*)
- Back panel/flap (piece No. 3): cut x 1 (*fabric 2*)
- Patch pocket (piece No. 4): cut x 1 (*fabric 1*)
- Lining, front panels (piece No. 1): cut x 2 (*lining*)

SUPPLIES

- 50cm (19¾in) fancy, shiny, printed fabric, composition 43% polyester, 33% acrylic, 24% metal (*fabric 1*)
- 50cm (19¾in) yellow toile (*fabric 2*)
- 50cm (19¾in) yellow poplin lining, 100% cotton (*lining*)
- 50cm (19¾in) thin iron-on interfacing
- 1 x 30cm (11¾in) gold zip in natural cotton
- Yellow thread

METHOD

‣Iron thin interfacing onto pieces 1 and 2 (*front and back, fabric 1*). Do not put any interfacing on the flap as this is thick (depending on which fabric is used).

MAKING A SIMPLE POCKET
step by step

PREPARING THE POCKET

‣Hem along the upper edge of piece No. 4 as follows: fold in 1cm (½in) all along the edge, then iron. Fold in 1cm (½in) for a second time all along then iron. Stitch 1mm ($1/32$ in) from the edge.
‣Turn in the other three sides 1cm (½in) and iron in the folds. **(1)**

‣Clip the corners of the bag. **(2)**

‣Place the pocket in the centre of the back lining in the position marked on the pattern and pin into place. Stitch around three sides of the pocket, 1mm ($1/32$ in) from the edge. Stitch round again, 5mm (¼in) from the first seam. **(3)**

SEWING THE MAIN BODY OF THE BAG TOGETHER

‣Align the flap (piece No. 3) with the back (piece No. 2), right sides together and stitch along this edge. Press the seam up, then topstitch 1mm ($1/32$ in) from the seam to hold the seam allowance in place.
‣Place the zip on the back panel, right sides together.
‣Lie the back lining on top, right sides together, sandwiching the zip between the two pieces of fabric.
‣Secure with pins then stitch. Repeat for the front panel (*see step by step Setting eyelets*).

step by step P. 12

‣Push the zip to the top (flat-mounted zip) and open it a little way.
‣Sew together the front and back panels of the bag, right sides together.

SEWING THE LINING

‣Sew together the front and back of the lining, right sides together, leaving an opening of around 10cm (4in) in the seam at the bottom.
‣Sew up the bottom of the bag by hand using slipstitch or by topstitching on the machine.

step by step

CREATING AN
EVEN TOPSTITCH

Shopping bag

Our inspiration for this bag comes from the attractive paper bags you get for your purchases from the big brands. In recent times, carrying an eye-catching shopping bag from one of the major retail outlets has become a fashion statement in itself, and this paper bag could certainly replace a handbag. This is why we wanted to use the basic shape of a shopping bag to make a fabric version. We have opted for a technical fabric, neoprene, which holds its shape and looks very up-to-date. As it is a reversible fabric, we have also used the wrong side of the fabric for the lining. A removable support piece at the bottom of the bag gives a bit more strength to the base. For the handles, simple rope tied off with knots at the ends will do the trick, but it must be sufficiently thick. The sort we have used reminded us of yachting ropes, but you can use any type. You could even recycle the cords from a paper shopping bag you have at home.

PATTERN PIECES

Fabric 1

‣ Front and back panels of the bag (piece No. 1):
cut x 1 on the fold (*fabric 1*)
‣ Lining (piece No. 2 to be cut along the line shown): cut x 1
fabric on the fold (used on the reverse side) (*fabric 1*)
‣ Bottom of bag (piece No. 3): cut x 2 (*fabric 1*)

SUPPLIES

‣ 1m (39½in) of double-sided neoprene, composition
82% polyester, 12% viscose, 6% elastane (*fabric 1*)
‣ Pink thread
‣ 1m (39½in) medium iron-on interfacing
‣ 50cm (19¾in) semi-rigid iron-on interfacing
‣ 4 large nickel eyelets
‣ 1.5cm (⅝in) diameter cord: 2 x 80cm (31½in)

METHOD

▸Cut out the pattern pieces from the fabric. Note: the pattern piece should be cut on the fold of the fabric. To do so, fold the fabric along the weft, place the edge of the pattern (marked 'fold') on the line of the fold and cut.

PREPARING THE REMOVABLE BASE SUPPORT

▸Place the pattern piece for the base of the bag (piece No. 3) on a piece of semi-rigid (plastic) iron-on interfacing and trace. Using a universal ruler, decrease the size of the piece by 1.25cm (½in) along each edge and cut out.
▸Cut pattern piece No. 3 from the medium iron-on interfacing.
▸On the ironing board, iron the semi-rigid plastic onto the wrong side of the fabric, ensuring that it is centred on the piece. Then iron the medium interfacing on top to fix everything in place.
▸Sew the pieces of fabric that form the base of the bag together, right sides facing, leaving an opening of 15cm (6in) along one of the long sides.
▸Turn the right side out, iron flat and turn the seam allowance in along the opening.
▸Sew the opening closed by hand using slipstitch.

CREATING AN EVEN TOPSTITCH — step by step

PREPARING THE OUTER FABRIC

▸Cut piece No. 1 from the medium iron-on interfacing and iron the interfacing onto the back of piece No. 1. **(1)**

▸Trace the fold lines with a ballpoint pen (refer to pattern). **(2)**

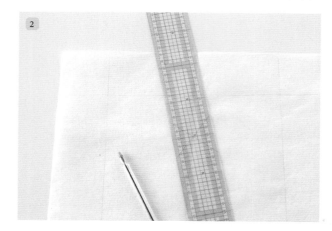

› Carefully cut along each fold line on the interfacing without cutting the outside fabric. **(3)**

› Using the sewing machine, stitch long lines on the wrong side of the piece, 0.5cm (¼in or ½ presser foot) from each fold. This ensures that each of the bag's folds is clearly marked and attractively highlighted by the topstitching. **(4)**

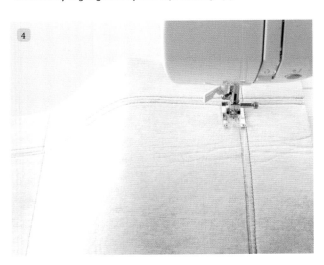

SEWING THE BAG TOGETHER

› Fold piece No. 1 along the fold line and sew together the front and back down each side, right sides together (pink side = right side). Oversew 1cm (½in) from the triangular cut-out on the edge.
› Fold so you can align the lower edges of the cut-out triangle where you have just finished stitching with the apex of the triangle below. Sew them together as in the diagram.

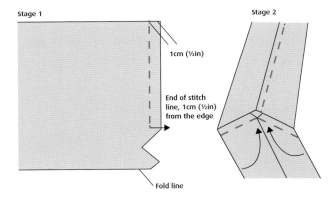

Stage 1   Stage 2

1cm (½in)

End of stitch line, 1cm (½in) from the edge

Fold line

› Sew the lining together in the same way (use the reverse side of the reversible fabric). Leave a 20cm (7¾in) opening on one of the sides of the lining.
› Sew the lining to the bag by pinning them right sides together. Stitch and turn the right way out through the opening you left in the side. Sew up the opening using slipstitch or the sewing machine.
› Fold over the top edge of the bag along the fold line and iron all the folds of the bag into place.

› Your bag is almost finished. Place the removable base support piece inside the bag. All that remains is to set the eyelets (see step by step Setting eyelets).

P. 40

› Finally, thread the cord through the eyelets (tie a knot at each end of the cord) to form the handles. Happy shopping!

ATTACHING BIAS
BINDING

step by step

Transparent tote

The materials used make this a very modern, original tote. The bag's finishings have been chosen to highlight the material and cut down as far as possible on stitching. The transparent outer material gave us the idea of adding a pocket which could display a photograph or a picture. The handles are looped and attached using snap fasteners. The inside consists of a removable lining made from a simple fabric pouch that ties shut with a cord. If want to use different materials, consider a coated fabric or vinyl, as this will allow you to leave the edges unfinished, otherwise you will need to add a seam allowance for the top of the bag and hem with a double turn over.

PATTERN PIECES

Fabric 1   Fabric 2

- Front and back panels (piece No. 1): cut x 2 (fabric 1)
- Gusset (piece No. 2): cut x 1 (fabric 1)
- Front and back pocket panels (piece No. 3): cut x 2 (fabric 1)
- Front and back lining (piece No. 1): cut x 4 (fabric 2)
- Gusset lining (piece No. 2): cut x 2 (fabric 2)
- Placket for drawstring eyelets (piece No. 4): cut x 1 (fabric 2)

SUPPLIES

- 1m (39½in) of transparent plastic (average weight) (fabric 1)
- 1m (39½in) grass-printed cretonne fabric, 100% cotton (fabric 2)
- 120cm (47¼in) folded black satin bias binding
- Black thread
- 2 black coated handles
- 8 x 1cm (½in) diameter nickel snap fasteners
- 2 nickel eyelets
- 150cm (59¼in) of 0.5cm (¼in) diameter cord
- Matching green thread
- 1 x 90 machine needle for heavy fabric

THE UNEXPECTED IN FASHION

In 1995, Armani created a transparent bag – a real window into the bag's contents, considered by most people to be an insight ino the person carrying it.

Since then, numerous designers have enjoyed creating fantasy versions of these day-to-day accessories: the Dali for Schiaparelli telephone bag, Nina Ricci chess piece bag and the perfecto or McDonalds bag from Moschino. A rite of passage for any contemporary stylist, bags are ideal objects to stimulate creation and an indispensable accessory when it comes to achieving new styles.

Totes
(continued)

METHOD

▸ Cut the pattern pieces from the materials; the number you need of each is given on the pattern.

ATTACHING BIAS BINDING
step by step

ATTACHING THE POCKETS

▸ Lie the front and back plastic panels flat and, referring to the pattern, lightly trace the two long straight stitch lines for the pockets, using the fine point of a propelling pencil.
▸ Use black thread to sew on the pockets along these lines.

SETTING THE SNAP FASTENERS

▸ Mark the location of the snap fasteners on the front and back with the propelling pencil.
▸ Put the male side of the studs on the bag.
▸ Make a hole in the handle material using a punch and a hammer, then tap on the female part.

SEWING TOGETHER THE BODY OF THE BAG

▸ Attach the gusset to the front and back (pieces 1 and 2), stitching 1cm (½in) from the edges. Ensure you make neat angles so the corners are well formed
(see step by step Sewing on a gusset with a corner).

P. 33

▸ Trim the seams to 0.7cm (¼in) so that the bias binding to be attached subsequently will cover the seams nicely. **(1)**

▸ Prepare the satin bias binding by carefully ironing the fold and stretching it slightly under the iron. **(2)**

▸ Fold along one edge and measure the place where the corner will be formed, then secure with pins to form the corner. Measure the distance to the next corner and proceed in the same way for the second corner. **(3)**

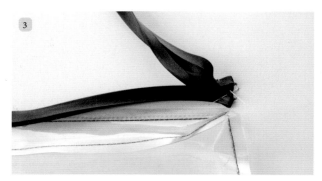

› Measure to the edge of the bag and oversew the bias binding at the top corner. **(4)**

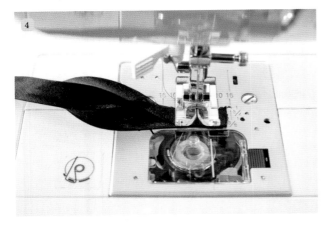

› Sew up the corners at the places marked using the sewing machine. Turn the bias binding the right way out and iron well.
› Sew on the bias binding 1mm ($^1/_{32}$ in) from the edge all round the bag, ensuring that it sits nicely over the edges so that it is even and does not become detached. **(5)**

› Proceed in the same way to attach the binding to the other edge.

SEWING TOGETHER THE REMOVABLE LINING

› Sew the inside bag together twice (because it is lined in the same material):
→ 2 x gussets and front panels, right sides together.
→ 2 x gussets and back panels, right sides together.
→ Note: leave an opening of around 20cm (7¾in) at the bottom of one of them.
› Sew the top edges together right round, right sides together, and turn the right way out. Sew up the opening using slipstitch or the sewing machine.
› Topstitch (see page 9) to hold the side of the lining nice and flat inside the bag. Then iron.
› Put the placket that will reinforce the fabric for the eyelets in place. Set the eyelets at the positions marked 4cm (1½in) apart.
› Draw a line using an erasable pen or tailor's chalk 3cm (1¼in) from the bag's top edge. Run the cord drawstring round the top of the bag and pin all around to keep it in place. Stitch along the line drawn around the bag: you have formed the drawstring casing. Tie knots at each end so the cord does not disappear into the casing.

MAKING HANDLES *step by step*

Big bag with pocket

We love this oversized tote bag which makes a fantastic holdall. In summer, it is perfect for trips to the seaside, but it also works well for shopping in town. Its flared shape is what makes it stand out. The size means it works well with a large print. An outside zipped pocket creates a compartment for your valuables. It is closed for safe keeping using three snap fasteners.

PATTERN PIECES

- Central panels of bag (piece No. 1): cut x 2 (*fabric 1*)
- Side panels of bag (piece No. 2): cut x 2 (*fabric 1*)
- Upper pocket panel (piece No. 3): cut x 1 (*fabric 1*)
- Lower pocket panel (piece No. 4): cut x 1 (*fabric 1*)
- Base of bag (piece No. 5): cut x 1 (*fabric 1*)
- Central facing (piece No. 3): cut x 2 (*fabric 1*)
- Side facing (piece No. 7): cut x 2 (*fabric 1*)
- Handles (piece No. 8): cut x 2 (*fabric 1*)
- Loops (piece No. 9): cut x 4 (*fabric 1*)
- Lining, central panels (piece No. 4): cut x 2 (*fabric 2*)
- Lining, side panels of bag (piece No. 10): cut x 2 (*fabric 2*)
- Lining, base of bag (piece No. 5): cut x 1 (*fabric 2*)

SUPPLIES

Fabric 1 *Fabric 2*

- 1m (39½in) two-tone urban spirit jacquard fabric (*fabric 1*)
- 1m (39½in) lining/black chintz (*fabric 2*)
- 1m (39½in) medium iron-on interfacing
- 50cm (19¾in) semi-rigid plastic iron-on interfacing for the base
- Black thread
- 1 x 30cm (11¾in) nickel zip, black
- 4 x 2.5cm (1in) long oval nickel rings
- 3 x 1cm (½in) diameter nickel snap fasteners

PLAYING WITH STRIPES

Remember, printed fabric = pattern match.

Even if it is not possible to precisely align the patterns, you can make the whole thing look good by choosing where to position the pattern pieces when cutting out the fabric. Try to align the pattern on the front pocket panels with the panels on either side.

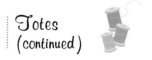

METHOD

▸ Cut the pattern pieces from the fabrics.
▸ Cut all the external pieces of the bag and the facings (apart from the handles and the base), namely pieces 1, 2, 3, 4 and 7, from medium iron-on interfacing and iron each of these pieces onto the wrong side of the fabric.

PREPARING THE BASE SUPPORT PIECE

▸ Place the pattern piece for the base of the bag (piece No. 5) on a piece of semi-rigid (plastic) iron-on interfacing and trace. Using a universal ruler, subtract 1.25cm (½in) along each edge and cut out.
▸ Cut pattern piece No. 5 from medium iron-on interfacing.
▸ On the ironing board, iron the semi-rigid plastic onto the wrong side of the fabric, ensuring that it is centred on the piece. Then iron on the medium interfacing to fix everything into place.

PREPARING THE EXTERNAL POCKET IN THE CENTRAL PANEL

▸ Sew on the zip between the lower and upper panels of the big front pocket (right sides together).
▸ Sew on the lining in the same way and if you can, topstitch (see page 9) along the lining edge to keep it in place and ensure that it does not get caught in the zip.
▸ To form the pocket bag, place piece No. 1 behind the pocket, pin in place (right side of piece No. 1 on to the wrong side of pieces 3 and 4) and sew right round, 0.5cm (¼in) from the edge.

MAKING HANDLES — step by step

PREPARING THE HANDLES

▸ Prepare the handles (piece No. 8) by folding them right sides together lengthways and sewing them up along the long side, 1cm (½in) from the edge. **(1)**

▸ Turn the right way out. You can use a knitting needle or wooden spoon handle to turn the bag handles out more easily. **(2)**

TIP

Use a washing-up glove to help you turn out the handles – the rubber sticks to the fabric better.

▸ Once you have turned the handles the right way out, iron flat.

TIP

Use a knitting needle or wooden spoon handle to open out and flatten the seams.

▸Topstitch the full length, 0.5cm (¼in) from each edge (width of half a presser foot). **(3)**

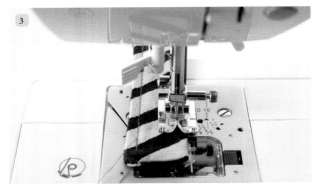

▸Stitch two more rows at the same distance between these two lines. **(4)**

PREPARING THE LOOPS AND THE RINGS

▸Fold the loop pieces right sides together, stitch and turn the right way out.

▸Use the handle of a wooden spoon to help you open out and flatten the seams.

▸Topstitch as you did for the handles.

▸Pass each loop through a ring and fold. **(a)** and **(b)**

▸Stitch to hold in place using a zipper foot. Hold the threads firmly as you start to sew (this prevents the machine from 'skating' when the fabric is too thick). **(c)**

▸Attach the loops at either end of the front and back panels, 1cm (½in) inside the seam with the side panels.

ASSEMBLING THE BODY OF THE BAG

▸Pin the front and back panels to the side panels right sides together (make sure they are the right way up) and sew together.

▸On the wrong side of the fabric, open out all the seams with an iron and clip the corners.

▸Pin the base to the edges, right sides together. Line up the notches to ensure the middles are properly aligned. Sew together.

TIP

To ensure the curved seam sits well, clip the seam allowance around the base. This will ensure the base sits better.

▸Assemble the facing pieces. Iron open the seams and clip the corners to reduce bulk.

▸Pin the bag to the facing, right sides together. Align the seam lines on the bag and the facing. Sew together.

▸Sew the lining pieces together, ironing open the seams and leaving an opening of around 30cm (11¾in) in the side of the bag.

▸Sew the lining and the facing together, right sides together.

▸Turn the right way out through the opening left in the side. Sew up the opening using slipstitch or the sewing machine. Your bag is almost ready. You just need to attach the handles.

▸Pass the handles through the rings and fold, 5cm (2in) from the end. **(d)**

▸Stitch a square as shown in the diagram (the cross in the middle is optional). **(e)**

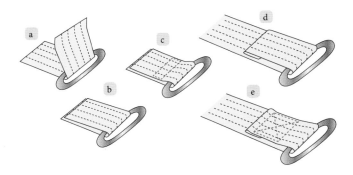

SEWING ON A
GUSSET WITH
A CORNER

step by step

Box bag

This little urban, printed bag is simple and practical whatever you are doing. It is worn over the shoulder and has a handy compartment pocket.

PATTERN PIECES

Fabric 1   *Fabric 2*

- Front and back panels (piece No. 1): cut x 2 (*fabric 1*)
- Gusset (piece No. 2): cut x 1 (*fabric 1*)
- Zip casing (piece No. 3): cut x 2 (*fabric 1*)
- Loops (piece F): cut x 2 (*fabric 1*)
- Shoulder strap (piece G): cut x 1 (*fabric 1*)
- Zip pull (piece No. 6): cut x 1 (*fabric 1*)
- Zip tabs (piece No. 7): cut x 2 (*fabric 1*)
- Zipped pocket (piece No. 8): cut x 2 (*fabric 1*)
- Front and back lining panels (piece No. 1): cut x 2 (*fabric 2*)
- Gusset lining (piece No. 2): cut x 1 (*fabric 2*)
- Zip casing lining (piece No. 3): cut x 2 (*fabric 2*)

SUPPLIES

- 50cm (19¾in) printed hemp graffiti fabric (broad width 280cm (110in), 70% cotton, 30% polyester (*fabric 1*)
- 50cm (19¾in) chick-yellow poplin (*fabric 2*)
- 50cm (19¾in) medium iron-on interfacing and thick interfacing
- 1 x 30cm (11¾in) nickel zip, black
- 2 x 2.5cm (1in)-wide rectangular nickel rings
- 1 x 2.5cm (1in)-wide adjustment buckle
- 1 x 18cm (7in) plastic spiral zip in complementary colour (here, orange)
- Black thread

METHOD

▸ Cut the pattern pieces from the fabrics.
▸ Iron interfacing onto the following pieces:
→ front and back panels of the bag with medium interfacing.
→ gusset with thick interfacing.
→ You could understitch round the pieces to keep the interfacing securely in place.

PREPARING THE INSIDE POCKET

▸ Here, the zipped pocket is a kind of zip-up purse that sits between the seams of the lining. The zipped pocket is cut from the same material as the bag (*fabric 1*) to make a nice contrast between the two fabrics. As a result, the zipped pocket will be inside the bag, with another compartment behind.
▸ First, attach the zip tabs in accordance with the diagrams below: bar tack the end of the zip to keep the ends together, prepare the tabs, then sew them to the ends of the zip, topstitching 1mm ($^1/_{32}$ in) from the end. **(1)**

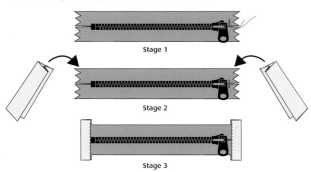

Stage 1

Stage 2

Stage 3

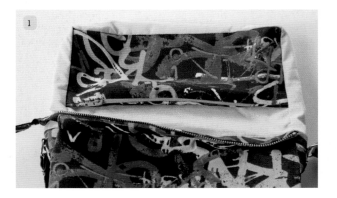

▸ Sew the zip to one pocket panel, right sides together, then take the other pocket panel and repeat the step (see step by step *Putting in a zip*).

P. 12

▸ Sew the front and back lining panels to the gusset, taking in the sides of the pocket in the seams between the back panel and gusset of the lining. Make sure you line up the top edges of the pocket well with both ends of the zip. Remember to leave an opening at the bottom of the lining so you can turn the bag the right way out.

PUTTING THE ZIP IN THE ZIP CASING

▸ Make a tab at the end of the zip using the diagrams below: fold the edges longways, clip the corners, fold the other corner, then fold in half, place round the end of the zip and topstitch 1mm ($^1/_{32}$ in) from the folded edges.

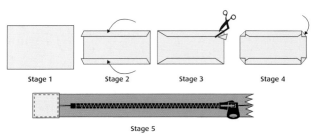

Stage 1   Stage 2   Stage 3   Stage 4

Stage 5

▸ Place the zip on the top of the zip casing, right sides together. Place the lining right sides together on top, trapping the zip between the two pieces.
▸ Sew up the ends of the two sides of the zip casing, then turn the zip casing the right way out so the zip is visible **(2)** (see step by step *Setting a zip in a zip casing*).

P. 36

PREPARING THE SHOULDER STRAP AND BUCKLE LOOP

▸For the shoulder strap and loops, (see step by step *Making handles*). step by step P. 28

▸Sew the loops onto the gusset of the bag on either side, inserting the ring.

 step by step SEWING ON A GUSSET WITH A CORNER

SEWING TOGETHER THE BODY OF THE BAG

▸It is often necessary to sew round a corner in bag making. We use this process several times in this book.
▸First line up the edges of the fabric, right sides together, and pin, then sew on the two panels. When you arrive at the corner (1cm or ½in) from the edge, clip up to the tip of the needle. **(3)**
▸Pivot the panel. **(4)**

▸Continue stitching until the next corner. **(5)**

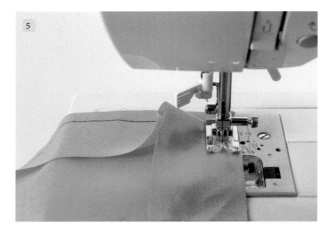

SEWING THE LINING TOGETHER

▸Sew the front and back panels of the lining to the gusset, then sew the lining and the body of the bag together, leaving an opening at the bottom. Turn the right way out.
▸Sew up the bottom of the lining by hand, or by topstitching on the sewing machine.

SETTING A ZIP IN
A ZIP CASING *step by step*

Courier bag with flap

This courier bag with a flap is a super-practical, everyday bag that is worn slung over the shoulder. It's suitable for every season, depending on the choice of fabric.

PATTERN PIECES

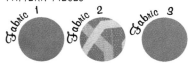

- Front and back panels (piece No. 1): cut x 2 (*fabric 1*)
- Flap (piece No. 2): cut x 2 (*fabric 2*)
- Gusset (piece No. 3): cut x 1 (*fabric 1*)
- Zip casing (piece No. 4): cut x 4 (*fabric 1*)
- Shoulder strap (piece G): cut x 1 (*fabric 2*)
- Loops (piece F): cut x 2 (*fabric 1*)
- Front and back panel lining (piece No. 1): cut x 2 (*fabric 3*)
- Gusset lining (piece No. 3): cut x 1 (*fabric 3*)
- Pocket window (piece D): cut x 1 (*fabric 3*)
- Pocket back (piece E): cut x 1 (*fabric 3*)

SUPPLIES

- 1m (39½in) printed, plain, linen-coloured fabric, 100% cotton (*fabric 1*)
- 50cm (19¾in) Zeva canvas, 61% polyester, 26% polyester, 13% linen (*fabric 2*)
- 50cm (19¾in) linen-coloured lining (*fabric 3*)
- 50cm (19¾in) medium iron-on interfacing
- 50cm (19¾in) thin iron-on interfacing
- 1 nickel flip-down clasp set
- 1 x 30cm (11¾in) separable zip, grey or beige
- 2 rectangular nickel loops, 2.5cm (1in) wide
- 1 x 18cm (7in) nickel pocket zip, grey or beige
- Beige or khaki thread

Courier bags
(continued)

METHOD

▸ Cut the pattern pieces from the fabrics.

PREPARING THE PIECES

▸ Iron medium interfacing onto the front/back panels and the gusset of the bag.
▸ Iron thin interfacing onto the flap.
▸ Iron thin interfacing onto the front and back lining, the pocket back and the pocket window piece.

MAKE THE POCKET WINDOW IN THE LINING

(See step by step Making a zipped pocket window.)

P. 93

step by step

step by step

SETTING A ZIP IN A ZIP CASING

PREPARING THE ZIP AND ZIP CASING

▸ Line up one side of the zip with one side of the zip casing (right side of the zip on right side of the fabric). Stitch along the full length. **(1)**

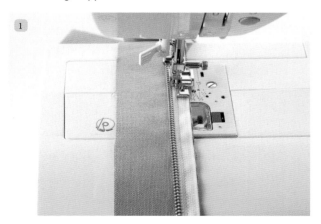

▸ Lie the zip casing lining on top, right side down, trapping the zip between the two pieces of fabric. **(2)**

▸ Follow the same process with the other side of the zip and the remaining two pieces of zip casing. Sew up the casing at each end. Turn the zip casings the right way out so the zip is visible. **(3)**

▸ Attach the two zip casings at the top of the bag. **(4)**

MAKING THE FLAP

- Sew the front and back of the flap together (sew round three sides, leaving the edge that will be topstitched to the bag open).
- Topstitch round three sides of the flap, 1mm ($1/32$ in) from the edge.
- Attach the clasp (female side) to the flap at the position shown on the pattern.

ATTACHING THE STRAP

(See step by step Making a shoulder strap.)

step by step P. 82

- Turn in 1cm (½in) along the full length.
- Fold the band of fabric in half lengthways, wrong sides together and press the fold (as for bias binding).
- Topstitch the length of the shoulder strap, 1mm ($1/32$ in) then 5mm (¼in) from the edges.
- Pass the band round the central adjustment buckle, fold and topstitch the end.
- Pass the band through the ring, back through the adjustment buckle and then the second ring. Fold back 5cm (2in), turn the end in and topstitch.

ASSEMBLING THE BODY OF THE BAG

- Sew the front and back panel to the gusset

(see step by step Sewing on a gusset with a corner).

step by step P. 33

- Put in the bottom of the clasp at the position shown on the pattern.
- Sew the flap to the back panel, along the top of the bag, taking the back panel and zip casing into the seam.
- Assemble the lining, leaving an opening at the bottom.
- Sew the lining to the body of the bag.
- Turn the right way out and sew up the opening using slipstitch or the sewing machine.

SETTING EYELETS

step by step

Duffel bag

This casual over-the-shoulder bag is drawn closed by a cord that is also the shoulder strap. We have chosen an ethnic fabric with a plain colour that highlights the pattern.

PATTERN PIECES

Fabric 1   Fabric 2   Fabric 3

- Lower front and back panels (piece No. 1): cut x 2 (*fabric 1*)
- Upper front and back panels (piece No. 1): cut x 2 (*fabric 2*)
- Base of bag (piece No. 3): cut x 1 (*fabric 1*)
- Removable inside pocket (piece No. 4): cut x 2 (*fabric 1*)
- Pocket zip tabs (piece No. 5): cut x 2 (*fabric 1*)
- Lining, base of bag (piece No. 3): cut x 1 (*fabric 3*)
- Lining, front and back panels (piece No. 1): cut x 2 (*fabric 3*)

SUPPLIES

- 1m (39½in) jacquard fabric, 81% polyester, 19% cotton (*fabric 1*)
- 1m (39½in) pink fabric (*fabric 2*)
- 1m (39½in) coral orange cotton poplin lining (*fabric 3*)
- 1m (39½in) medium iron-on interfacing
- 50cm (19¾in) thin iron-on interfacing
- 50cm (19¾in) thick iron-on interfacing
- 10 large nickel eyelets
- 1 x thick cord, 1cm (½in) diameter
- 1 x 20cm (7¾in) matching zip
- 2 x 1cm (½in) diameter nickel or black snap fasteners
- Pink thread

METHOD

‣ Cut the pattern pieces from the fabrics.
‣ Iron thin interfacing onto the lower front and back pieces. Iron thick interfacing onto the round base and the upper panels.

MAKING THE INSIDE POCKET

‣ Attach the zip tabs (piece No. 5) by the method given for the courier bag, page 32.
‣ Bar tack the end of the zip to keep the ends together, prepare the tabs, then sew them to the ends of the zip, topstitching 1mm ($\frac{1}{32}$ in) from the edge.
‣ Prepare two lengths of bias binding the length of the zip in the lining fabric and stitch them along both parts of the zip. Set the zip (see step by step Putting in a zip).
‣ Mark the position of the snap fasteners and set the two snap fasteners on the back panel of the pocket. P. 12
‣ Mark the position of the snap fasteners and set the two snap fasteners on the bag lining.
‣ Sew together the front and back of the pocket, right sides together.

PREPARING THE UPPER PART

‣ Sew the sides of the upper pieces (pink fabric) together.
‣ Fold the cylindrical shape formed by the upper part and iron in the fold. Then set the eyelets.

SETTING EYELETS
step by step

SETTING EYELETS

‣ Mark the position of the eyelets with an erasable pen. Mark the centre of the eyelet (take the eyelet, place it in the correct position and draw round the inside of it). **(1)**
‣ Cut out the circle with the tips of your scissors. **(2)**

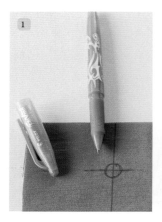

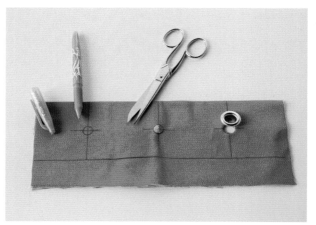

- Place the upper part of the eyelet in this hole, then position the lower part underneath. **(3)**
- Use the tool that comes with the kit and a hammer to set the eyelet. **(4)**

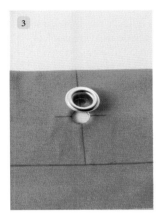

SEWING TOGETHER THE BODY OF THE BAG

- Sew up the side seams, then press the seams open with an iron.
- Sew together the upper part **(fabric 2)** and the lower part (piece No. 1), lining up the seam markers.

Note: only one thickness of the upper part should be taken into the seam as the other side will be sewn to the lining.

- Sew in the round base of the bag, then clip all round.
- Sew together the front and back lining, right sides together, leaving an opening on one side so you can turn the bag the right way out, then iron open the seams.
- Sew the lining on to the folded-over inside edge of the top of the bag, turn the right way out, then sew up the opening in the side.

step by step

MAKING A POCKET CASING

Bucket bag

A duffel-style bag that you can carry in your hand or over your shoulder. It's the contrasting materials and colours that make it really striking.

PATTERN PIECES

Fabric 1   Fabric 2   Fabric 3

- Upper panels of the bag, front and back (piece No. 1): cut x 2 (fabric 1)
- Lower panels, front and back (piece No. 2): cut x 2 (fabric 2)
- Base (piece No. 3): cut x 1 (fabric 2)
- Lining, front and back panels (piece No. 4): cut x 2 (fabric 3)
- Lining, base of bag (piece No. 3): cut x 1 (fabric 3)
- Upper part zip pocket (piece A): cut x 2 (fabric 3)
- Lower part zip pocket (piece B): cut x 2 (fabric 3)
- Pocket back (piece C): cut x 1 (fabric 3)
- Top of handle (piece No. 8): cut x 1 (fabric 1)
- Underside of handle (piece No. 9): cut x 1 (fabric 2)

SUPPLIES

- 1m (39½in) black velour, 54% acrylic, 28% cotton, 12% polyester, 6% viscose (fabric 1)
- 50cm (19¾in) mock-croc imitation leather (fabric 2)
- 1m (39½in) printed vintage cretonne lining, 100% cotton (fabric 3)
- 50cm (19¾in) medium iron-on interfacing
- 1 x 15cm (6in) gold zip, white
- 4 large gold eyelets
- 2 gold magnetic snap fasteners
- 2 x 2.5cm (1in)-wide gold snap hooks
- 50cm (19¾in) rigid iron-on interfacing
- Black thread

BAG FOR BUBBLES

This style of bag was invented originally by the Louis Vuitton fashion house for the purpose of carrying bottles of champagne.

METHOD

▸ Cut out the pieces from the materials.

MAKING A POCKET CASING — step by step

PREPARING THE BODY OF THE BAG

▸ Iron medium interfacing onto pieces 1 and 3.
▸ Sew together the sides of pieces 1 and 2.
▸ Sew the upper and lower parts of the outer bag together: the imitation leather base is sewn to the body of the bag. To do so, mark the position of the base and sew, right sides together.
▸ Fold the seam allowances down and topstitch 0.5cm (½in) from the edge of the gold material to make sure they are well secured.
▸ Assemble the base of the round bag, lining up the markers. Clip the seam allowance all round the base of the bag to make it easier to stitch round.
▸ Fold over the facing and iron in the fold.
▸ Mark the positions of the magnetic fasteners and put them in place (see step by step *Attaching magnetic snap fasteners*).

P. 78

MAKING THE POCKET

▸ Bar tack the end of the zip to keep the edges together.
▸ Lay the zip face down (right sides together) on piece A.
▸ Lay the other half of the zip face down (right sides together) on piece B. **(1)**
▸ If you are confident at sewing, you could fold over the pocket opening, so the zip is set in a 'casing'.
▸ Place the pocket back (Piece C) right sides together with parts A and B **(2)**. Sew all round, leaving the top edge open **(3)**. Clip the corners, turn the right way out and iron. **(4)**
▸ Sew the pocket to the top edge of the lining panel.

PREPARING THE LINING

▸ Sew together the front and back lining panels, leaving an opening around 20cm (7¾in) along one of the sides.
▸ Sew on the round base of the lining and clip it.
▸ Sew the upper part of the lining to the upper part of the bag, right sides together. Turn the right way out through the opening left in the side. Sew up using slipstitch or the sewing machine.

▸ Mark the position of the eyelets and set them in place (see step by step *Setting eyelets*).

P. 40

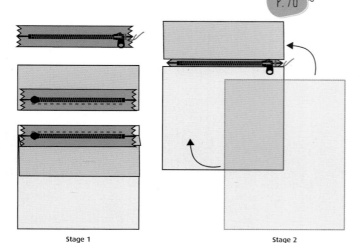

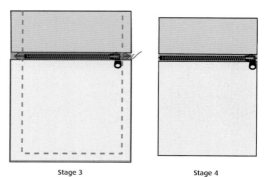

Stage 1   Stage 2   Stage 3   Stage 4

PREPARING THE HANDLE

▸On piece No. 8, fold in 1cm (½in) along each edge.

▸Align piece No. 9 edge to edge.

▸Pass piece No. 8 through the snap hook, then fold it back under the imitation leather for 4cm (1½in).

▸Stitch 1mm (¹/₃₂ in) from the edges.

▸As you approach the snap hook, stitch and turn when you get around 1cm (½in) from the ring. As the foot does not let you get right up to the snap hook ring, you need to backstitch a few stitches.

Clip the snap hooks through the bag eyelets, from one side to another, to finish your bag.

Waist bag

BEGINNER LEVEL

MAKING A PATCH POCKET WITH A FLAP — step by step

Waist bag

This is a relaxed bag you can carry anywhere, especially when travelling. Its unusual shape and the novel way you wear it meant it had to be included in our collection. It is also a unisex bag.

PATTERN PIECES

Fabric 1   Fabric 2

▸ Front and back panels of bag (piece No. 1): cut x 2 (*fabric 1*)
▸ Front pocket (piece No. 2): cut x 2 (*fabric 1*)
▸ Pocket flap (piece No. 3): cut x 2 (*fabric 1*)
▸ Waist strap (piece No. 4): cut x 2 (*fabric 1*)
▸ Loops for attaching strap (piece No. 5): cut x 2 (*fabric 1*)
▸ Decorative fringe (piece No. 6): cut x 1 (*fabric 1*)
▸ Lining, front and back panels (piece No. 1): cut x 2 (*fabric 2*)

SUPPLIES

▸ 1m (39½in) world map printed canvas, 100% cotton (*fabric 1*)
▸ 50cm (19¾in) palm-leaf patterned cotton, 100% cotton (*fabric 2*)
▸ 50cm (19¾in) iron-on wadding/batting
▸ 2 x 25cm (9¾in) matching zips
▸ 1 x 2.5cm (1in)-wide bronze buckle with prong
▸ 6 small brass eyelets
▸ 1 sew-on snap fastener
▸ Small transparent or bronze sew-on snap fasteners
▸ Beige thread

A HOLIDAY FEEL

Fashionable among tourists in the 1990s, this type of bag has fallen out of fashion for a while, but here it has been brought bang up to date.

Waist bag (continued)

MAKING A PATCH POCKET WITH A FLAP

step by step

PREPARING THE POCKET

▸ Sew the darts on the two pocket pieces (piece No. 2).
▸ Sew the two pieces right sides together, lining up the darts and leaving an opening between the two of them. Mitre the corners. **(1)**

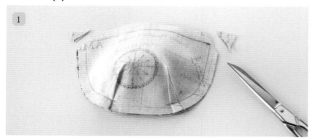

▸ Turn the right way out and iron.
▸ Topstitch 1mm ($\frac{1}{32}$in) and 0.6cm (¼in) along the straight edge, see diagram above right.
▸ Sew together the pocket flap, piece No. 3, right sides together, leaving an opening along the straight top edge. Mitre the corners. **(2)**

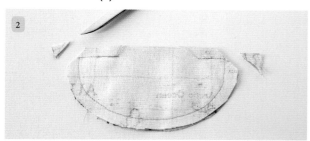

▸ Turn the right way out and iron flat.
▸ Topstitch 1mm ($\frac{1}{32}$in) and 0.6cm (¼in) round the curved edges, see diagram above right.
▸ Pin the pocket onto the body of the bag as marked and stitch 1mm ($\frac{1}{32}$in) from the edge all round the pocket. Pivot the pocket and stitch round again 0.6cm (¼in) from the first stitch line.

POCKET TOPSTITCHING WAIST BAG

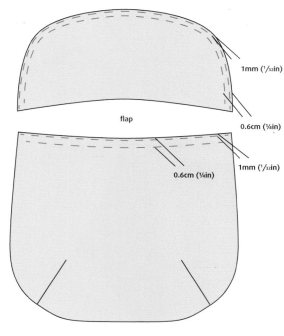

flap

1mm ($\frac{1}{32}$in)

0.6cm (¼in)

0.6cm (¼in)

1mm ($\frac{1}{32}$in)

pocket

▸ Pin the flap onto the body of the bag as marked and stitch 1mm ($\frac{1}{32}$in) from the edge along the top straight edge of the flap. Bend it over and stitch another line 0.6cm (¼in) from the first stitch line. **(3)**
▸ Sew on small snap fasteners to close.

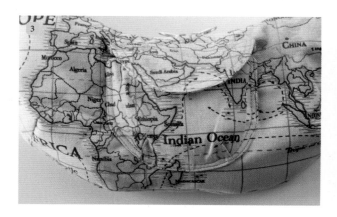

PREPARING THE BELT

▸Fold in 1cm (½in) along each long edge of pieces No. 4 and iron flat.
▸Fold the ends of the belt as shown in the following diagram.
▸Place the two bands on top of each other and oversew 1mm (¹⁄₃₂in) from the edges.

PREPARING THE LOOP FOR THE BUCKLE AND PRONG

▸Fold in 1cm (½in) along the long edges of pieces No. 5 and iron flat.
▸Place the two bands on top of each other and oversew 1mm (¹⁄₃₂in) from the edges.
▸Fold in half and pass through the buckle.
▸Mark the position of the prong and cut a 0.5cm (¼in) slit with the point of your scissors.
▸Pass the prong through and iron flat.

MAKING THE DECORATIVE FRINGE

▸Fold in 1cm (½in) all along the long edge of piece No. 6 and iron flat.
▸Fold edge to edge and sew 1mm (¹⁄₃₂in) from the edge.
▸Cut as many fringe strands as you want and finish them with a little knot.
▸Place them side by side along one of the edges of the bag, ready to sew on. **(4)**

ASSEMBLING THE BODY OF THE BAG

▸Sew the small darts.
▸Place the two zips right sides together on each side of the bag, ensuring that the zip stops are aligned with the marker in the middle of the bag.
▸Sew in the lining and topstitch (see page 9) so that it lies flat on the inside of the bag.
▸Sew on the loop and the pronged buckle at one side, carefully centred, allowing it to extend 1cm (½in) beyond each end (see pattern). Sew the bag together, right sides together, over the loop.
▸Attach the waist strap in the same way on the other side.
▸Place the decorative fringes next to the loop on the lower part of the bag.
▸Sew round the bottom of the bag.
▸Sew up the lining in the same way, leaving a 20cm (7¾in) opening in the bottom. Turn the right way out and sew up the opening using slipstitch or the sewing machine.

Small sports bag

We have created this easy-to-sew bag based on the sports bag project. The fabric used makes it extra special. It can be carried over the shoulder using handles made from shiny synthetic strapping that looks a bit like grosgrain ribbon. You can accentuate the sporty-chic, or make it more casual, depending on the fabric you use.

PATTERN PIECES

- Front and back panels (piece No. 1): cut x 2 (*fabric 1*)
- Side panels (piece No. 2): cut x 2 (*fabric 1*)
- Side pockets (piece No. 3): cut x 2 (*fabric 1 on the fold*)
- Lining, front and back panels (piece No. 1): cut x 2 (*fabric 2*)
- Lining, side panels (piece No. 2): cut x 2 (*fabric 2*)

SUPPLIES

- 1m (39½in) geometric blue jacquard, 100% polyester (*fabric 1*)
- 1m (39½in) blue chintz lining (*fabric 2*)
- 50cm (19¾in) iron-on wadding/batting
- Black polyester strapping, 2 x 110cm (43¼in), width 4cm (1½in)
- 1 x 40cm (15¾in) plastic zip, black
- Navy blue or black thread

Cylindrical bags
(continued)

METHOD

▸ Cut out the pieces from the materials. Note that piece No. 3 (side pockets) should be cut on the fold, i.e. you need to fold the fabric in half and line up the fold lines of the pattern and the fabric.

▸ Iron the wadding/batting onto outside fabric pieces 1 and 2. This will give the bag shape and keep it 'inflated'.

PREPARING THE EXTERNAL END POCKETS

▸ Mark the position of the snap fastener on the round side piece using tailor's chalk or an erasable pen.

▸ Attach the male side of the snap fastener.

▸ Fold pieces No. 3 along the fold line marked on the pattern.

▸ Mark the position of the snap fastener on the pocket piece using tailor's chalk or an erasable pen.

▸ Attach the female side of the snap fastener.

▸ Lie the right side of the No. 2 pieces on the wrong side of the No. 3 pieces and sew all round, 0.7cm (¼in) from the edge.

ASSEMBLING THE BODY OF THE BAG

▸ Sew the zip to the outer fabric.

Note: Leave a 2cm (¾in) gap at the beginning and end of the zip to make it easier to sew on the side panels later.

▸ Sew the side lining panels along the zipped edge of the outer fabric, right sides together.

ATTACHING STRAPS

step by step

▸ Mark the position of the straps in tailor's chalk. **(1)**

▸ Sew the strapping to each side. **(2)**

▸ If you want, you can finish the stitch line that attaches the handles with a square, as shown in the diagram on page 53. **(3)**

▸ Sew up the base of the bag, ensuring that the straps are precisely aligned. **(4)**

▸ Sew the round ends to the front and back panels, right sides together.
▸ Sew the lining panels together: front and back panels (leave a 20cm (7¾in) opening at the bottom of the bag) and side panels to the front and back panels.
▸ Turn the right way out and sew up the opening using slipstitch or the sewing machine.

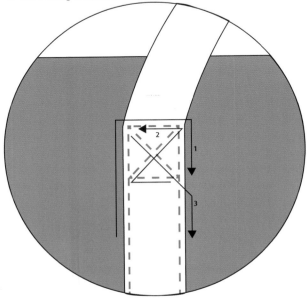

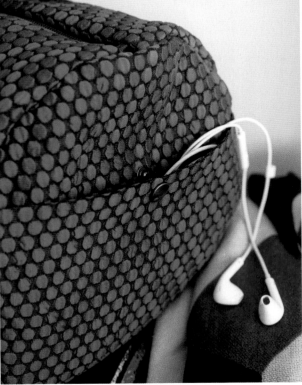

Cylindrical bags
CONFIDENT

ATTACHING PIPING — step by step

MAKING HANDLES — step by step

PREPARING A BASE SUPPORT PIECE — step by step

Travel bag

The shape of this bag is very familiar, and the finished product means it is not just a handbag but a really classy travel bag too. Its retro look is part of its charm. Technically speaking, it requires attention to detail to achieve a polished finish. The trickiest bits are the base of the bag, the handles, the handle tabs, the straps on the end pieces and the piping.

PATTERN PIECES

Fabric 1   Fabric 2

- Front and back panels (piece No. 1): cut x 2 (*fabric 1*)
- Side panels (piece No. 2): cut x 2 (*fabric 1*)
- Base (piece No. 3): cut x 2 (*fabric 2*)
- Side straps (piece No. 4): cut x 2 (*fabric 2*)
- Shoulder strap (piece No. 5): cut x 2 (*fabric 2*)
- Tabs for the zip ends (piece No. 6): cut x 2 (*fabric 1*)
- Tabs for the handles (piece No. 7): cut x 8 (*fabric 2*)
- Handles (piece No. 8): cut x 2 (*fabric 2*)
- Lining, front and back panels (piece No. 1): cut x 2 (*lining*)
- Lining, side panels (piece No. 2): cut x 2 (*lining*)
- Lining, base of bag (piece No. 3): cut x 1 (*lining*)
- Pocket above the zip (piece A): cut x 2 (*lining*)
- Pocket below the zip (piece B): cut x 2 (*lining*)
- Pocket back (piece C): cut x 1 (*lining*)

SUPPLIES

- 1m (39½in) red toile (*fabric 1*)
- 1m (39½in) red imitation leather (*fabric 2*)
- 1m (39½in) red chintz lining (*lining*)
- 1 x 35cm (13¾in) gold zip, red
- 6 gold 'D' rings
- 2 gold snap hooks
- 4 gold bag feet (attached like split pins)
- 1m (39½in) medium iron-on interfacing
- 50cm (19¾in) semi-rigid iron-on interfacing
- 1 x 18cm (7in) spiral zip, red
- 1m (39½in) of cord, approximately 1cm (½in) in diameter
- Red thread
- 1 x 90 machine needle for heavy fabric
- Fabric glue
- Clothes pegs

A BIT OF HISTORY

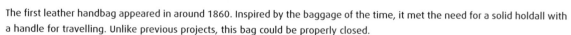

The first leather handbag appeared in around 1860. Inspired by the baggage of the time, it met the need for a solid holdall with a handle for travelling. Unlike previous projects, this bag could be properly closed.

It is impossible to talk of the birth of the handbag without mentioning the emancipation of women: they no longer required a man to carry their belongings: they could look after their own affairs and their money.

Cylindrical bags
(continued)

METHOD

▸ Cut out the pieces from the materials.
▸ Iron medium interfacing onto the outer bag pieces.

ATTACHING THE STRAPS FOR THE SIDES

▸ Mark the position of the straps on the side panels using tailor's chalk or an erasable pen, following the pattern.
▸ Fold in 1cm (½in) along the long edges of the strap and glue down to ensure the fabric remains in place.
▸ Pass it through the rings and then turn under 5cm (2in).
▸ Sew a large cross on this part (see page 53).
▸ Sew the straps to each side of the bag, so that that the top end where the ring sits has 2cm (¾in) play. **(1)**

see page 53

ATTACHING PIPING

step by step

ATTACHING PIPING

▸ For the piping, cut a 3cm-wide (1¼in) band of imitation leather across the whole width. Prepare the piping by folding the strips of material in half and slipping the piping cord into the fold. Sew in place. **(2)**

▸ Cut, leaving a seam allowance of 1cm (½in). **(3)**

▸ Sew the piping round the side panels (piece No. 2) using the zipper foot of the sewing machine.
▸ To turn a corner, sew up to the corner, then lower the needle into the material, clip the corner and pivot the material and piping so you can start on the next side. **(4)**

▸ Turn the end of the piping in before and after you get to the strap, so it is not too bulky. **(5)**

ATTACHING THE HANDLE TABS

‣Sew together 2 x No. 7 pieces **(stages 1 and 2)**.
‣Cut as shown in **stage 3** and turn the right way out.
‣Topstitch as shown in **stage 4**.
‣Draw lines at 6cm (2¼in) and 6.5cm (2½in) in erasable pen.
‣Fold round the rings.
‣Mark the positions of the handle tabs on the body of the bag using tailor's chalk or erasable pen.
‣Place the handle tabs with the rings on the bag and stitch round 1mm ($^1/_{32}$ in) from the edge, and then 6mm (¼in) from the edge and along the lines drawn at 6cm (2¼in) and 6.5cm (2½in). **(6)**

MAKING HANDLES

‣Draw the 1cm (½in) seam allowance all along.
‣Apply double-sided adhesive tape or fabric glue, fold and finger press to hold in place. **(7)**

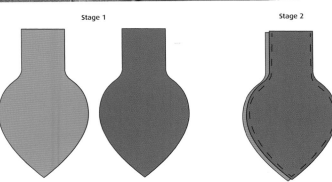

Stage 1　　　　Stage 2　　　　Stage 3　　　　Stage 4

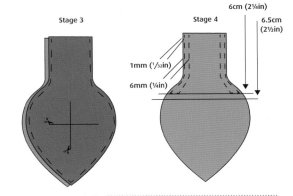

6cm (2¼in)
6.5cm (2½in)
1mm ($^1/_{32}$in)
6mm (¼in)

Cylindrical bags
(continued)

- Topstitch in the same way as for the handle tabs (see diagram on page 57).
- 5cm (2in) from the end, fold over the rings. **(8)**

- Place a thick cord in the centre and glue into place. **(9)**

- Glue and fold the long edges together, holding them in place with clothes pegs. **(10)**

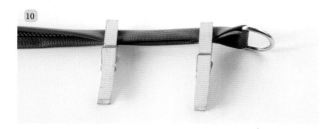

- Sew 1.5mm (¹⁄₁₆in) from the edges using the machine's zipper presser foot. **(11)**

PREPARING A BASE SUPPORT PIECE

PREPARING A BASE SUPPORT PIECE FOR THE OUTER BAG

- Cut the base piece (piece No. 3) from plastic semi-rigid iron-on interfacing and trim, taking off 1.25cm (½in) all round.
- Cut the same piece from some medium iron-on interfacing.
- First iron the semi-rigid interfacing onto the reverse of the fabric, ensuring that it is carefully centred, then iron on the medium interfacing with the edges aligned.
- Sew a large cross between the corners of the piece you have made to hold the materials in place. **(12)**

- Mark the position of the feet with a pen.
- Make holes using a punch and a hammer. **(13)**

▸ Fold in 1cm (½in) along the long edge, stick down the stitch allowance (using double-sided adhesive tape or fabric glue) and finger press to hold in place. **(14)**

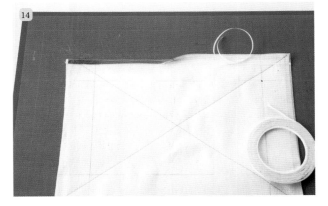

▸ Fix the bag feet at the positions marked.

ASSEMBLING THE BODY OF THE BAG

▸ Attach the zip to the outer fabric and place the lining under the zip.
▸ Place a tab folded in four at each end of the zip and stitch.
▸ Sew the inner base of the bag to the front and back panels.
▸ Sew the outer base of the bag to the already sewn inner base, 1mm (¹⁄₃₂ in) from the edge. **(15)**

▸ Sew up the side panels, making sure that the markers are carefully aligned.
▸ Stitch in the base of the lining, leaving an opening of around 30cm (11¾in).
▸ Stitch in the side panels of the lining.
▸ Turn the right way out and sew up the opening using slipstitch or the sewing machine.

ADDING THE SHOULDER STRAP

▸ Fold in 1cm (½in) along the long sides of the pieces of fabric, and glue down.
▸ Stitch 1mm from the edges and finish as close as possible to the rings.
▸ Pass the ends through the rings and fold over 5cm (2in) from the ends.
▸ Finish with a square (see page 53).

You can also add an inside pocket using pattern pieces A, B and C. You could for example follow the pocket instructions for the bucket bag, page 44.

Bowling bag

INTERMEDIATE LEVEL

MAKING A LEATHER-STYLE SHOULDER STRAP *step by step*

Bowling bag

Here we have aimed for a neo-modernist take on the little sporty number – a bag with bags of personality. Based on a bowling bag, it is small and lightweight, and you wear it casually over the shoulder with a strap. The trickiest thing about this project is that the materials used are hard and form a thick layer under the machine's presser foot. On the plus side, you do not need to use iron-on interfacing for the bag to keep its shape.

PATTERN PIECES

Fabric 1   Fabric 2   Lining

- Front and back panels (piece No. 1): cut x 2 (*fabric 1*)
- Gusset (piece No. 2): cut x 1 (*fabric 2*)
- Top panels (piece No. 3): cut x 2 (*fabric 2*)
- Loops for rings (piece No. 4): cut x 2 (*fabric 2*)
- Top side of strap (piece No. 5): cut x 1 (*fabric 2*)
- Underside of strap (piece No. 6): cut x 1 (*fabric 2*)

- Front and back lining panels (piece No. 1): cut x 2 (*lining*)
- Gusset lining (piece No. 2): cut x 1 (*lining*)
- Lining, top panels (piece No. 3): cut x 2 (*lining*)
- Pocket window (piece D): cut x 1 (*lining*)
- Pocket back (piece E): cut x 1 (*lining*)

SUPPLIES

- 50cm (19¾in) geometric print imitation leather (*fabric 1*)
- 50cm (19¾in) Karia plain maroon imitation leather, 76% polyester, 22% polyester, 2% polyurethane (*fabric 2*)
- 1m (39½in) black and white checkerboard (*lining*)
- 1 x 30cm (11¾in) nickel zip, maroon
- 2 x 2cm (¾in) diameter nickel rings
- 2 x 2.5cm (1in) diameter nickel snap hooks
- 1 x 13cm (5in) plastic spiral zip, black
- Maroon thread
- 1 x 90 machine needle for heavy fabric

Bowling bag
(continued)

METHOD

▸ Cut out the pieces from the materials.

MAKING A
LEATHER-STYLE
SHOULDER STRAP

step by step

PREPARING THE SHOULDER STRAP AND THE LOOPS FOR THE RINGS

▸ Fold in 1cm (½in) along the long edges of piece No. 5 and stitch 0.5cm (¼in) from the edges. **(1)** and **(2)**

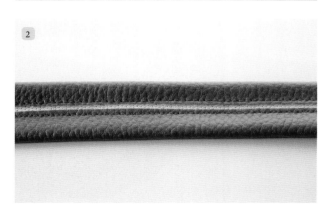

▸ Place piece No. 6 on top, wrong sides together.

▸ Topstitch 1mm (¹/₃₂ in) from the edges. **(3)**

▸ Do the same to make the loops. Pass each loop through a ring. Then stitch across as close to the ring as possible. Position each loop at the place marked on piece No. 2 (gusset). **(4)**

▸ Pass each end of the long strap through a snap hook and fold over 5cm (2in) from the end. Sew across as close as possible to the snap hook and finish the stitching. **(5)**

PREPARING THE INSIDE POCKET

▸ Set the zip in the zip window
(*see step by step Making a zipped pocket window*).

P. 93

ASSEMBLING THE BODY OF THE BAG

▸ Put in the zip on top of the bag
(*see step by step Putting in a zip*).
P. 12

▸ Attach the lining and topstitch (see page 9).
▸ Sew together the lower part of the bag: the gusset of the bag is complete.
▸ Finish sewing the lining together: sew the gusset and the front and back panels leaving an opening of around 20cm (7¾in) at the bottom of the bag.
▸ Now assemble the gusset of the bag around the front and back panels, aligning the markers carefully (pivot to sew round the corners)
(*see step by step Sewing on a gusset with a corner*).
P. 33

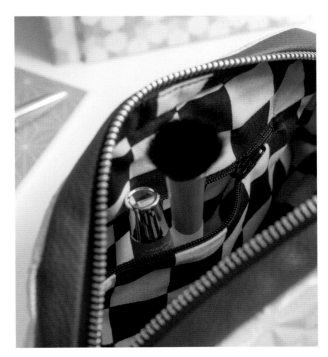

▸ Make sure that as you go round the corner, you clip carefully while the needle is down through the fabric.
▸ Turn the bag the right way out and sew up the opening using slipstitch or the sewing machine.
▸ Attach the shoulder strap using the small snap hooks. You can also make a zip pull by folding a narrow strip of imitation leather. This will give the bag a leatherwork look. **(6)**

Small shoulder bag

This project is made of imitation leather which has a soft finish on the reverse, so that it also works as lining (which makes the task much easier!). As a result, the finishings are quite simple. The shoulder strap gives some added interest: it is a single long strap that goes round the bag like a belt.

PATTERN PIECES

> Front and back panels (piece No. 1): cut x 2 (fabric 1)
> Gusset (piece No. 2): cut x 1 (fabric 1)
> Flap (piece No. 3): cut x 2 (fabric 1)
> Strap loops (piece No. 4): cut x 2 (fabric 1)
> Shoulder strap (piece No. 5): cut x 2 (fabric 1)

SUPPLIES

> 1m (39½in) dragon imitation leather, white and silver, 84% PVC, 14% polyester, 2% polyurethane (fabric 1)
> 2m (79in) bias binding, gold
> 1 brass magnetic snap fastener
> 1 brass buckle with prong, width 2.5cm (1in)
> 3 brass eyelets
> White thread
> 1 x 90 machine needle for heavy fabric

THE SHOULDER BAG

Coco Chanel raided the functionalism of the masculine world to transgress genres and transform the military kit bag: 'Tired of carrying my bags in my hands and losing them, I added a strap and slung them over my shoulder.'

Towards the end of the 1930s, Elsa Schiaparelli created over-the-shoulder satchels that were adopted on a massive scale by French women who were obliged to travel by bicycle during the Occupation.

METHOD

▸Cut out the pieces from the materials.

ATTACHING THE MAGNETIC SNAP FASTENER

▸Mark the position of the snap fastener with an erasable pen.
▸Attach the snap fastener: male side on the inside of the flap, female side on the front panel
(see step by step Attaching magnetic snap fasteners).

step by step P.78

PREPARING THE GUSSET

▸Make the loops: fold in 1cm (½in) along the long edges of piece No. 4. Cut this piece into three equal sections (see pattern) and topstitch on the right side 0.6cm (¼in) from the edge.
▸Mark their position on the gusset band as shown on the pattern.
▸Lay the loops across the gusset band and sew them on 0.7cm (just over ¼in) from the edge. **(1)**

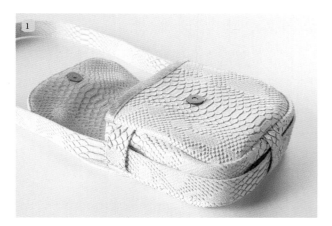

PREPARING THE SHOULDER STRAP

▸Lay shoulder strap pieces No. 5 wrong side to wrong side and stick together using double-sided adhesive tape or fabric glue.
▸Stitch 1mm ($^1/_{32}$in) from the edges.
▸Pass one end through the pronged buckle, fold over 5cm (2in) from the end and sew.
▸Cut a small slit with the point of your scissors for the prong.

▸At the other end of the shoulder strap, mark the position of the eyelets with an erasable pen. Make holes using a punch and hammer and set the eyelets. **(2)**

MAKING THE FLAP

▸Put the flap together by sewing the two No. 3 pieces together, right side to right side, leaving a 10cm (4in) opening along the top straight edge (the edge that will be sewn on to the back panel).
▸Clip the seam allowances round the curved edges, mitre the corners and turn the right way out. **(stage 1)**
▸Mark the position of the flap on the back of the bag with an erasable pen and stitch 1mm ($^1/_{32}$in) and 0.6cm (¼in) from the edges. **(stages 2 and 3)**

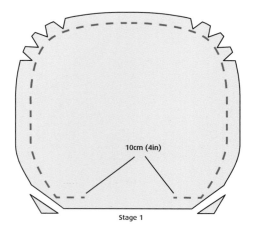

10cm (4in)

Stage 1

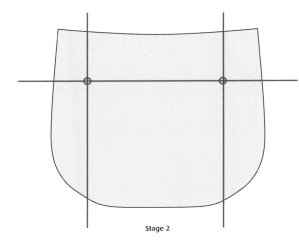

Stage 2

SEWING TOGETHER THE BODY OF THE BAG

▸ Attach the bias binding to the top edge of the front panel
  (piece No. 1).
▸ Sew the front and back to the gusset, right sides together.
▸ Finish the bag by adding bias binding all round the seam
  allowances, starting at the bottom of the bag. **(3)**

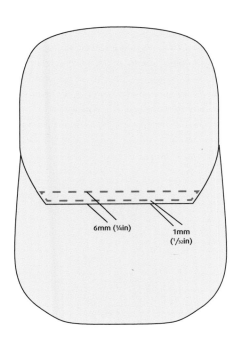

6mm (¼in)

1mm
(¹/₃₂in)

Stage 3

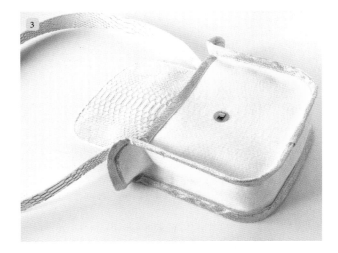

Studded shoulder bag

This bag is fastened using snap fasteners concealed under the straps. The studs really create its appeal and the suedette fabric contrasts well with the cotton strapping.

PATTERN PIECES

- Front and back panels (piece No. 1): cut x 2 (*fabric 1*)
- Gusset (piece No. 2): cut x 1 (*fabric 1*)
- Flap (piece No. 3): cut x 2 (*fabric 1*)
- Lining, front and back panels (piece No. 1): cut x 2 (*fabric 2*)
- Lining, gusset (piece No. 2): cut x 1 (*fabric 2*)

SUPPLIES

- 1m (39½in) navy blue suedette (*fabric 1*)
- 50cm (19¾in) flamingo-print cotton, 100% cotton (*fabric 2*)
- 1m (39½in) iron-on wadding/batting
- 50cm (19¾in) medium iron-on interfacing
- 2m (79in) navy blue cotton strapping, width 2.5cm (1in)
- Brass studs, 2 boxes x 20 studs
- Metallic gold piping, 2 x 65cm (25½in)
- 2 gold-coloured brass magnetic snap fasteners
- Matching navy blue thread

METHOD

▸Cut out the pieces from the materials.
▸Iron medium interfacing on to the front and back panels of the bag (pieces No. 1).
▸Iron medium interfacing on to the gusset of the bag (piece No. 2).

PREPARING THE FLAP

▸Mark the position of the straps on the top side of the flap, using tailor's chalk.
▸Sew on the straps leaving 10cm (4in) overlap at the bottom (for the magnetic snap fasteners).
▸Attach the studs to the flap: pierce the suedette with the studs on the right side, then open out the prongs on the reverse side.
▸Cut the flap piece from the wadding/batting and iron it on to the back of the top panel of the flap (this will make it thicker and give the flap a padded look).
▸Sew together the front and underside of the flap using a zipper presser foot around three sides, mitre then turn the right way out.

ATTACHING THE MAGNETIC SNAP FASTENERS

▸Attach the top parts of the fasteners to the straps.
▸Attach the bottom parts of the fasteners to the bag. **(1)**

ASSEMBLING THE BODY OF THE BAG

▸Sew the piping round the front and back panels (pieces No. 1) using a zipper foot (see step by step Attaching piping). P.56

▸Sew the gusset of the bag to the front, then the back, right sides together.
▸Mark the position of the flap and sew it onto the back panel of the bag.
▸Attach the shoulder strap to the sides, turn under 3cm (1¼in) at each end and topstitch at 1mm ($^1/_{32}$in) and 3cm (1¼in). **(2)**

ASSEMBLING THE LINING

▸Assemble the lining: sew the lining gusset (piece No. 2) to the front and back of the lining (piece No. 1), leaving an opening at the bottom of the bag.
▸Align the lining with the top of the bag, right sides together, and stitch.
▸Topstitch the lining (see page 9) so that it sits flat inside the bag.
▸Turn the right way out and sew up the opening using slipstitch or the sewing machine.

Safari bag

The flap on this bag is a large zip pocket. It has two big snap hooks. Its casual look and bold print inspire thoughts of far-flung holidays.

PATTERN PIECES

- Front and back panels (piece No. 1): cut x 2 (fabric 1)
- Gusset (piece No. 2): cut x 1 (fabric 1)
- Flap (piece No. 3): cut x 2 (fabric 2)
- Shoulder strap (piece G): cut x 1 (fabric 2)
- Lining, front and back panels (piece No. 1): cut x 2 (fabric 3)
- Lining, gusset (piece No. 3): cut x 1 (fabric 3)
- Flap (piece No. 3): cut x 2 (fabric 3)

SUPPLIES

- 1m (39½in) chocolate suedette (fabric 1)
- 50cm (19¾in) striped, patterned jacquard, 64% polyester, 36% cotton (fabric 2)
- 50cm (19¾in) mustard-yellow cotton voile, 100% cotton (fabric 3)
- 50cm (19¾in) medium iron-on interfacing
- 1 x 60cm (23½in) nickel zip, chocolate brown
- 1 x 1cm (½in) diameter end ring
- 1 nickel and imitation suede tassel
- 2 large nickel eyelets
- 2 x 3cm (1¼in) diameter round snap hooks
- 1 x 2.7cm wide (1⅛in) nickel adjustment buckle
- Brown thread

Shoulder bags
(continued)

METHOD

▸Cut out the pieces from the materials.
▸Iron wadding/batting onto the front and back panels (pieces No. 1) and gusset of the bag (piece No. 2).

PREPARING THE FLAP

▸Place the zip round the flap, right sides together, then stitch.
▸Place the flap lining under the zip and stitch.
▸Place the tassel on the zip. **(1)**

ASSEMBLING THE BODY OF THE BAG

▸Assemble the front and gusset of the bag, right sides together.
▸Assemble the back and gusset of the bag, right sides together. Take care at the point where the gusset of the bag meets the front and back (see Shopping bag diagram, page 21).
▸Pin the flap to the back part of the bag, then sew it on.
▸Lining: assemble the front, back and gusset lining in the same way as the external fabric (leaving an opening at the bottom of the bag).
▸Align the lining with the top of the bag, stitch, turn the bag the right way out and sew the opening closed using slipstitch or the sewing machine.

SETTING THE EYELETS

▸Set the two eyelets on either side of the bag, ensuring they go right through all the layers (see step by step Setting eyelets).

ATTACHING THE STRAP
(See step by step Making a shoulder strap.)

P. 40

P. 82

▸Turn in 1cm (½in) along the full length.
▸Fold the band of fabric in half lengthways, and iron in the fold (like bias binding).
▸Pass the band round the central bar of the adjustment buckle, fold and topstitch the end.
▸Pass the band through the snap hook, back through the adjustment buckle and then through the second snap hook. Fold back 5cm (2in), turn the end in and topstitch. **(2)**

ATTACHING MAGNETIC SNAP FASTENERS — step by step

Kelly bag

This classic accessory, made famous by Grace Kelly, inspired us to create this yellow version. The interfacing is essential to give it a good shape.

PATTERN PIECES

Fabric 1   Fabric 2

- Front and back panels (piece No. 1): cut x 2 (*fabric 1*)
- Side panels of bag (piece No. 2): cut x 2 (*fabric 1*)
- Base (piece No. 3): cut x 1 (*fabric 1*)
- Flap (piece No. 4): cut x 2 (*fabric 1*)
- Handle (piece No. 5): cut x 2 (*fabric 1*)

- Front and back lining panels and zip pocket panels (piece No. 1): cut x 4 (*fabric 2*)
- Lining, side panels (piece No. 6): cut x 4 (*fabric 2*)
- Lining, base of bag (piece No. 7): cut x 2 (*fabric 2*)

SUPPLIES

- 1m (39½in) mustard upholstery fabric, 62% polyester, 20% polyamide, 18% acrylic (*fabric 1*)
- 1m (39½in) pineapple-print lining, 100% cotton (*fabric 2*)
- 2 gold magnetic snap fasteners
- 1 x 25cm (10in) gold zip (lining pocket), white or natural cotton
- Yellow thread

THE KELLY BAG

This 'saddle bag' was first designed by the Hermès fashion house in 1892. It was later reworked and renamed the 'Kelly bag' in 1956 when the sublime American actress, Grace Kelly, who became Princess Grace of Monaco, appeared on the cover of *Life* magazine, holding the famous accessory. In a reference to our consumer society and the current fad for 'It bags', the French sculptor Sylvie Fleury raised this bag to the rank of work of art by casting it in bronze. This sculpture was then sold at the Drouot Auction House in Paris for a princely sum.

Trapezium bags (continued)

METHOD

▸ Cut out the pieces from the materials.
▸ There is no need for interfacing on this bag because the two fabrics used are thick.

PREPARING THE LINING

▸ The lining of the Kelly bag has three compartments, one of which closes with a zip.
▸ Put in the zip
(see step by step Putting in a zip).

step by step P. 12

▸ Then take the pocket now formed between the side panels of the lining into the seam (pieces No. 6).
▸ Assemble the front and back of the lining (pieces No. 1).
▸ Assemble the whole thing with the base (leaving an opening at the bottom of the bag so it can be turned the right way out).

ATTACHING MAGNETIC SNAP FASTENERS
step by step

ATTACHING A MAGNETIC FASTENER

▸ Mark the position of the magnetic snap fastener on the front of the bag (piece No. 1) with an erasable pen. **(1)**

▸ Make a slit with the point of your scissors (a tiny slit will do) so the prongs of the fastener can be pushed through the fabric. **(2)**

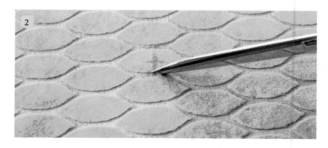

▸ Push the prongs of the fastener through and put the metal plate underneath to hold the prongs in place. **(3)**

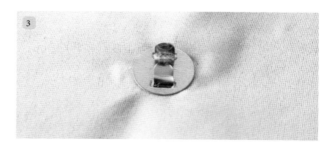

▸ Repeat with the other part of the snap fastener (male side) on each side of the flap (pieces No. 4). **(4)**

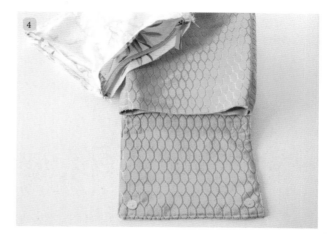

PREPARING THE HANDLE

▸ Turn in 1cm (½in) along each side.
▸ Fold the handle in half, like bias binding, and iron flat.
▸ Topstitch at each end.

PREPARING THE FLAP

▸ Sew the underside of the flap to the top side, right sides together
  (leave the top edge open, it will be sewn to the bag later).
▸ Mitre the corners, clip the curves, turn the right way out and
  iron flat.
▸ Attach the handle to the flap, sewing on a square. To sew the
  square, refer to the Sport's bag diagram, page 53.
▸ Sew up the back of the flap with topstitching 1.5mm (¹/₁₆in)
  from the edge and continue topstitching all round the flap.
▸ Stitch the flap to the back of the bag over the previous
  topstitching, 0.5mm (¹/₆₄in) away from it.

ASSEMBLING THE BODY OF THE BAG

▸ Sew the front and back to the sides then the base of the bag.
▸ Align the lining with the top of the bag, right sides together,
  pinning into place so you can sew the front and then the back
  in two stages: sew the bag round one side and then the other
  because the zip pocket can make the process tricky.
▸ Turn the bag the right way out through the opening left in the
  bottom of the bag, then sew up the opening using slipstitch or
  the sewing machine.

MAKING A
SHOULDER STRAP AND
ATTACHMENT LOOPS

step by step

Trapeze bag

A practical bag, perfect for carrying files and for general day to day use. The two outside faces are different and the lining will be sewn in the same fabrics.

PATTERN PIECES

- Middle panels front and back (piece No. 1): cut x 1 (*fabric 1*) x 1 (*fabric 2*)
- Flanking panels (piece No. 2): cut x 2 (*fabric 1*) x 2 (*fabric 2*)
- Side pieces (piece No. 3): cut x 2 (*fabric 2*)
- Base (piece No. 4): cut x 1 (*fabric 2*)
- Loops (piece F): cut x 2 (*fabric 2*)
- Shoulder strap (piece G): cut x 1 (*fabric 2*)
- Front and back lining panels (piece No. 7): cut x 2 (*fabric 1*)
- Lining, side pieces (piece No. 3): cut x 2 (*fabric 1*)
- Lining, base of bag (piece No. 4): cut x 1 (*fabric 1*)
- Patch pocket lining (piece No. 8): cut x 1 (*fabric 2*)

SUPPLIES

- 1m (39½in) black and white ethnic upholstery fabric (*fabric 1*)
- 1m (39½in) maroon toile (*fabric 2*)
- 1m (39½in) medium iron-on interfacing
- 1 gold magnetic snap fastener
- 6 gold 'D' rings
- 1 gold sliding adjustment buckle
- 2 gold magnetic snap fasteners
- 2 snap hooks
- Maroon thread

Trapezium bags
(continued)

METHOD

▸ Cut out the pieces from the materials.
▸ There is no need for interfacing on this bag because the two fabrics used are thick.

MAKING A
SHOULDER STRAP AND
ATTACHMENT LOOPS

step by step

MAKING A SHOULDER STRAP AND ITS ATTACHMENT LOOPS

▸ Prepare the shoulder strap: fold in 1cm (½in) along each side, fold the band of fabric in half like bias binding and iron flat.
▸ Topstitch the length of the shoulder strap, 1mm ($\frac{1}{32}$in) then 5mm (¼in) from the edges.
▸ Insert one end of the strap into the snap hook, fold back 5cm (2in) and fold under twice. Stitch across the turned end. **(1)**

▸ Pass the strap through the sliding buckle over the central bar and through the snap hook.
▸ Form a loop by passing the other end round the central bar of the closing buckle. Fold back 5cm (2in) and turn under twice then stitch round the turned end as close as possible to the sliding buckle. **(2)**

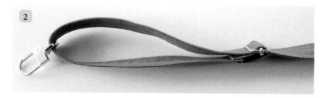

▸ To prepare the loops, follow the same process as for the strap.
▸ Insert the ring, sew the loop on at the point marked on the pattern. Fold then sew in a square to secure both ends. **(3)**

FORMING THE INSIDE POCKET

▸ Prepare and align the patch pocket, centred on the lining (*see step by step Making a simple pocket*).

step by step **P. 16**

▸ Attach the magnetic snap fastener to the No. 7 pieces (lining, front and back middle panels)

(*see step by step Attaching magnetic snap fasteners*).

step by step **P. 78**

ASSEMBLING THE BODY OF THE BAG

▸ Sew together the three front panels and the three back panels. Note that the colours are reversed: Panel 1: plain fabric, patterned fabric, plain fabric. Panel 2: patterned fabric, plain fabric, patterned fabric.

- Open out the seams, then topstitch 0.5cm (¼in) from each side of the seams on all the panels.
- Sew on the bag's side panels (pieces No. 3).
- Sew on the base of the bag (make sure you line up the notches because the base of the bag is wider than the side panels). Clip and pivot as you sew it to the front and back panels. **(4)**

ASSEMBLING THE LINING

- Sew the front and the back panel to the side panels.
- Sew to the base of the bag (leave an opening at the bottom of the bag for turning).
- Pin the lining to the top of the bag, right sides together, then stitch.
- Turn the bag the right way out through the opening left in the bottom, then sew closed using slipstitch or the sewing machine.

PADDING A FLAP · step by step

Chanel – style bag

This is in the style of one of the most iconic bags in the history of fashion, and features a padded flap. It is relatively easy to make, and this fresh look at an old classic combines the elegance of a shiny velour flap with the sporty look of its textured neoprene base.

PATTERN PIECES

Fabric 1   Fabric 2   Fabric 3

- Front panels (piece No. 1): cut x 1 (fabric 1)
- Back panels (piece No. 2): cut x 1 (fabric 1)
- Gusset (piece No. 3): cut x 1 (fabric 1)
- Underside of flap (piece No. 4): cut x 1 (fabric 2)
- Top side of flap (piece No. 5): cut x 1 (fabric 2)
- Lining, front and lining panels (piece No. 1): cut x 2 (fabric 3)
- Lining, gusset (piece No. 3): cut x 1 (fabric 3)
- Pocket window (piece D): cut x 1 (fabric 3)
- Pocket back (piece E): cut x 1 (fabric 3)

SUPPLIES

- 50cm (19¾in) textured neoprene (fabric 1)
- 50cm (19¾in) black velour (fabric 2)
- 50cm (19¾in) printed cotton twill lining, 100% cotton (fabric 3)
- 50cm (19¾in) iron-on wadding/batting
- 50cm (19¾in) thin iron-on interfacing
- 50cm (19¾in) semi-rigid iron-on interfacing
- 1 x 125cm (49¼in) gold chain
- 2 gold magnetic snap fasteners
- 2 large gold eyelets
- 2 small black snap fasteners
- 1 black plastic spiral zip, 13–15cm (5–6in) in length
- Black thread

THE CHANEL 2.55 BAG

The famous handbag, in leather or jersey, with its padded design, was directly inspired by the chequerboard jackets worn by grooms at the racecourse. Since it was first created in 1955, thanks to the creative verve of Karl Lagerfield, this type of bag has been produced in numerous forms: denim, raffia, sponge, straw, vinyl, gold and fluorescent, giant and tiny... There are around 180 steps involved in its manufacture!

Chic bags
(continued)

METHOD

▸ Cut the pattern pieces from the materials; the number that you need of each is given on the pattern.

PADDING A FLAP *step by step*

PREPARING THE FLAP

▸ Iron one piece of thin interfacing to the underside of the flap (piece No. 5).
▸ Mark the position of the magnetic snap fasteners on the underside of the flap (they must not be visible on the outside).
▸ Iron three layers of iron-on wadding to the underside of the flap (piece No. 4). The thicker the padding, the more attractive the flap will look. **(1)**

▸ Using the quilting ruler, draw parallel diagonal lines, 4cm (1½in) apart on the top side of the flap. Then draw lines perpendicular to the first series, again 4cm (1½in) apart. You now have a regular grid pattern. **(2)**

▸ Sew along the lines you have drawn (you need not start again at each new line, you can simply stitch, turn the fabric and then sew along the edge until you reach the next line, 4cm (1½in) away). The top side of the flap is now padded. **(3)**

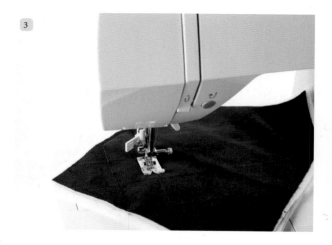

▸Sew onto the underside of the flap, which is not padded, stopping 1.25cm (½in) before the line where it will be attached to the main body of the bag and clip here.

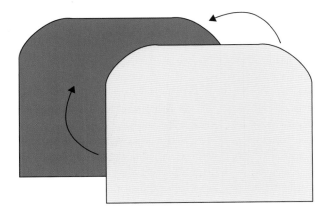

▸Mark the position of the eyelets and set the eyelets in the flap, ensuring that they pass through all the layers. **(4)**

PREPARING THE POCKET IN THE LINING

▸Make a pocket window

(see step by step *Making a zipped pocket window*).

 step by step P. 93 *step by step*

▸Assemble the rest of the lining (front and back panels and gusset, pieces 1 and 2) leaving an opening of around 20cm (7¾in) in the seam at the bottom.

ASSEMBLING THE BODY OF THE BAG

▸Iron two layers of thin interfacing onto the gusset of the bag (piece No. 3).
▸Prepare two pieces of thin interfacing for the front and back panels. Cut 2 x pieces 1 and 2 in a semi-rigid plastified interfacing, trimming off 1.25cm (½in) all round. Iron the band of semi-rigid interfacing between the two pieces of thin interfacing, ensuring that it is centred. Stitch this support round the front and back panels 0.7cm (¼in) from the edge. This will ensure the bag keeps its shape.
▸Turn under 1cm (½in) along the straight edge of the top part of the flap and topstitch to the back of the bag at the markers (do not take the underside of the flap into the seam!) 1mm (¹/₃₂in) and 0.5cm (¼in) from the edges.

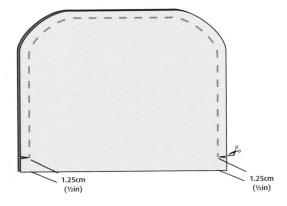

1.25cm (½in)   1.25cm (½in)

SEWING THE BAG TOGETHER

› Sew on the gusset. Take particular care with the corners of the bag under the flap on the back: the end point of each seam must be at exactly the same place.
› Attach the snap fasteners to the sides of the gusset at the position shown on the pattern.
› Sew on the lining and turn the right way out.

Note: when you get to the flap, the lining is taken into the seam with the underside.

› Through the hole in the lining, topstitch (see page 9) the inside of the bag, to ensure the lining lies flat.
› Sew up the opening in the lining using slipstitch or the sewing machine.

The bag is finished. You simply need to add the chain. Just open up the ring at one end and attach it to the ring at the other end using pliers, as explained in the Simple zip-up bag project on page 13.

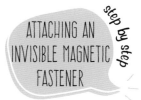

ATTACHING AN INVISIBLE MAGNETIC FASTENER — step by step

MAKING A ZIPPED POCKET WINDOW — step by step

Envelope bag

We imagined an envelope and then devised a bag along the same lines. It can be carried as a clutch or using a chain. We have chosen a grey and blue palette to highlight its interesting design.

PATTERN PIECES

 *Fabric 1* *Fabric 2* *Fabric 3* *Lining*

- Front panel – lower section (piece No. 1): cut x 1 (*fabric 1*)
- Front panel – upper section (piece No. 2): cut x 1 (*fabric 2*)
- Back panel of bag (piece No. 3): cut x 1 (*fabric 1*)
- Gusset (piece No. 4): cut x 1 (*fabric 1*)
- Top side of flap (piece No. 5): cut x 1 (*fabric 3*)
- Underside of flap (piece No. 6): cut x 1 (*fabric 3*)
- Facing (piece No. 7): cut x 2 (*fabric 1*)
- Loops for rings (piece No. 8): cut x 2 (*fabric 1*)

- Lining, front and back panels (piece No. 9): cut x 2 (*lining*)
- Gusset lining (piece No. 10): cut x 2 (*lining*)
- Lining, base of bag (piece No. 11): cut x 1 (*lining*)
- Pocket window (piece D): cut x 1 (*fabric 3*)
- Pocket back (piece E): cut x 1 (*lining*)

SUPPLIES

- 50cm (19¾in) navy blue suedette (*fabric 1*)
- 50cm (19¾in) silver artificial leather, 55% polyurethane, 45% viscose (*fabric 2*)
- 50cm (19¾in) taupe upholstery fabric, 62% polyester, 20% polyamide, 18% acrylic (*fabric 3*)
- 50cm (19¾in) printed lining (*lining*)
- 2 x 1cm (½in) diameter small nickel rings
- 2 x nickel snap hooks for the chain
- 105cm (41¼in) nickel chain
- 1 x 15cm (6in) separable nickel zip, black or navy
- 1 invisible snap fastener
- 1m (39½cm) medium iron-on interfacing
- 50cm (19¾in) thin iron-on interfacing
- Navy blue thread

METHOD

▸ Cut the pattern pieces from the fabrics.

PREPARING THE PIECES

▸ Iron medium interfacing on to the gusset of the bag (piece No. 4).
▸ Iron medium interfacing on to the front, back and flap (pieces 1, 2, 3, 5, 6).
▸ Iron thin interfacing onto the pocket window piece, the pocket back, and the linings (pieces 9, 10, and 11 and D and E).

ATTACHING AN INVISIBLE MAGNETIC FASTENER

▸ Mark the position of the fastener on the wrong side of the lining as shown on the pattern.
▸ Stick the fastener in place with a dab of glue or piece of double-sided adhesive tape.
▸ Using a zipper foot, sew right round it in a circle. **(1)** and **(2)**

› Follow the same process to attach the other part of the fastener to the underside of the flap (piece No. 6). **(3)**

PREPARING THE FLAP

› Assemble the underside and top side of the flap (pieces 5 and 6).

Note: do not sew up the sides of the flap right to the end but stop 1cm (½in) from the edge of the flap that will be sewn to the bag and notch.

› Mitre the corners.
› Turn the right way out and topstitch (see page 9) the flap up to the notch.

PREPARING THE FRONT OF THE ENVELOPE

› Sew together the two front panels in fabrics 1 and 2 (pieces 1 and 2).
› Clip at the point, then turn to finish sewing together.
› Topstitch.

MAKING A POCKET WINDOW ON THE BACK OF THE ENVELOPE

› Place the pocket window piece (piece D) on the back of the bag, right sides together (piece No. 3).
› On the window, use an erasable pen to draw a box (take the dimensions of the zip and draw a centred box in the window piece). In the box, draw a central horizontal 'reserve' line and small diagonals into the corners. **(stage 1)**

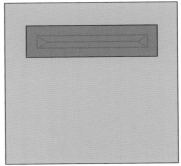

Stage 1

› Sew round the outline of the box you have drawn (only round the rectangle). **(stage 2)**

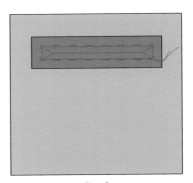

Stage 2

Cut along the reserve line and the small diagonals. **(4)**

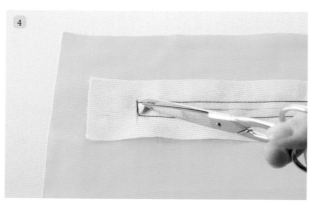

Turn the pocket window piece through to the back, then iron flat. **(5)**

Sew on the zip down both sides, taking the window piece and zip tape into the seam (but not taking in the main panel). **(stage 4)**

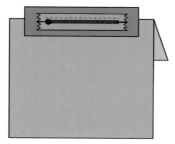

Stage 4

Sew along the diagonals on the zip and the window piece, still without taking in the main panel. **(stage 5)**

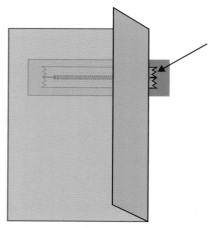

Stage 5

Sew on the folded pocket back, only taking the window piece, the zip and the lining into the seam, sewing over the previous seam lines (see arrows) **(stage 6 and photo 6)**.

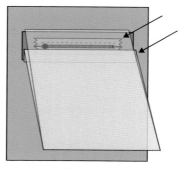

Stage 6

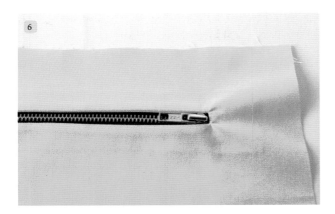

PREPARING THE LOOPS FOR THE RINGS

- Turn in 1cm (½in) along each side of the loops (piece No. 8).
- Fold the band of fabric in half lengthways, and iron, like bias binding.
- Topstitch along the edges, 1mm (¹⁄₃₂in) from each side.
- Mark the position of the rings on the gusset of the bag (piece No. 4) as shown on the pattern.
- Insert the ring, fold and stitch the loops (the snap hooks will clip on here).

ASSEMBLING THE BODY OF THE BAG

- Sew the underside of the flap to the back panel.
- Attach the gusset to the front and back.
- Sew together the sides of the two facing pieces.
- Align the facing with the top of the bag and sew (include the underside of the flap along the back).
- Topstitch all round the top of the bag.
- Assemble the front and back lining and the gusset, leaving an opening of around 15cm (6in) at the bottom.
- Sew together the lining and the facing (right sides together).
- Turn the bag the right way out through the opening in the bottom.
- Sew up the lining using slipstitch or the sewing machine.

First published in Great Britain in 2019

Search Press Limited
Wellwood, North Farm Road,
Tunbridge Wells Kent TN2 3DR

Original title: *J'apprends à coudre des sacs*
© 2016 by Éditions Marie Claire-Société d'Information et de Créations (SIC)

English translation by Burravoe Translation Services

French edition:
Director of publishing: Thierry Lamarre
Editor: Adeline Lobut
Editing/proofreading: Isabelle Misery

Creation, development and explanations: Estelle Zanatta, Marion Grandamme
Photographs: Fabrice Besse
Styling: Sonia Roy
Graphic design and lay-out: Either studio
Cover: Either studio

ISBN: 978-1-78221-556-1

Printed in Italy by G. Canale & C. Spa